Frog Praises Night
Poems with Commentary

By F. Richard Thomas

Southern Illinois University Press
Carbondale and Edwardsville
Feffer & Simons, Inc.
London and Amsterdam

Copyright © 1980 by Southern Illinois University Press
All rights reserved
Printed in the United States of America
Designed by Richard Neal

Library of Congress Cataloging in Publication Data

Thomas, F   Richard.
    Frog praises night.

    I. Title
PS3570.H5626F7   811'.5'4   79-22296
ISBN 0-8093-0959-9

For my father, Franklin A. Thomas (1909–1978)

Contents

Acknowledgments

"Millard Buckman" appeared in *Poetry Now*, 2:1 (1975); "Dream (for Gary C.)"; appeared in *Wind/Literary Journal* (Fall 1977); "Lee Ann" appeared in *Fadge* (Spring 1974) and in *Red Cedar Review*, 9:1 (Spring 1974); "Friends (for John Barnie)" appeared in *Beloit Poetry Journal*, 26:3–4 (Spring-Summer 1976); "My Brother, Born Dead" appeared in the anthology *The Day After Yesterday*, 1971; "We Are Forcing Forsythia" appeared in *The Windless Orchard Calendar 1973* (January 1973) and in *Notations*, 6 (1975); "For Sherry" appeared in *Streets* (November-December 1978); "Things" appeared in *Centering: A Magazine of Poetry 1*, (1973); "Marital Bliss" and "Nobody will Talk About My Poem" appeared in *Happiness Holding Tank* (Fall 1979); "Omen" appeared in *The Mississippi Valley Review*, 3:1 (Winter 1974) and in *Centering*, 1 (1973); "For My Son" appeared in *Centering*, 3 (1977); "Nikstlitslepmur" appeared in *Poetry Now* 4:1 (Spring 1978) and in *University College Quarterly* (Spring 1977); "Myself, My Home, The Moon" appeared in *Indiana Writes* (Fall 1976); "The Dream" appeared in *Star-Web Paper* (Spring 1973); "This Office" appeared in *Streets* (November-December 1978); "The Awakening" appeared in *Stoney Lonesome* (Winter 1978); "On Reincarnation and Related Matter" appeared in *Centering*; 1 (1973); "A Poem" appeared in *Fault*, 6 (November 1974); "The Soft Repose of Is" appeared in *Stoney Lonesome* (Winter 1978); and "Frog Praises Night" appeared in *Bits* (July 1976).

I would also like to thank the MacDowell Colony, Peterborough, New Hampshire; and the Department of American Thought and Language at Michigan State University for providing me with the time to complete this project; and Christoph Lohmann, Director, Graduate Program in American Studies, for offering a faculty appointment that provided excellent working conditions during my sabbatical year at Indiana University.

East Lansing, Michigan   Richard Thomas
August 17, 1979

The Poetry Reading

In the poetry reading poems come alive, become more accessible, because the poet is *there* with anecdotes, stories, tidbits. In a reading we become aware of the process as well as the product. To provide the flavor of a reading in this book I have supplied my own comments. Some of them are internal monologues, and others have become prose poems. But all are given simply for the purpose of enriching the original poems.

The poems existed before the concept of this book. Nevertheless, I have not attempted to exclude difficult poems. Rather, with the help of the forewords and afterwords to the poems, I hope untrained readers may better understand the ingredients of poetry—metaphor, ambiguity, mystery. As for experienced readers, I hope they will find the comments as interesting as those they might hear at a reading.

Why one would want to do this, why one would want to broaden the audience for poetry, is probably related to a personal, though not original, credo: In my experiences as a teacher I have learned that most enmity and fear of others is based on ignorance of what others think and feel. We tend to imagine those we don't understand as either more than human or less than human. What better way for me to reveal my humanness to others than through a reading of poems inspired by some of the people who have meant the most to me: my friends, my loved ones, my self.

Frog Praises Night

Sunset Bridge (a dream)

> For Franklin A. Thomas, 2/2/09–5/2/78.
> Poem written, 12/77.

As arranged,
we meet at Sunset Bridge
thirty years ago;
or, rather, you are thirty years younger,
and I the age I am now.
I'm surprised
by the mud road,
your long wool coat
and limp grey fedora;
surprised that we talk
near a deserted band shell
on a crumbling concrete bench,
the yellow sky threatening.

I tell you, Dad,
I tell you:
you must not smoke;
you mustn't eat so much;
you are dying of cancer
thirty years from now.

Why do you smile
as if you already know,
or don't care?
Perhaps I shouldn't have come
to tell you how urgent this is.

You don't understand the words
chemotherapy, radiology, cobalt, cytoxin.
You grin.

This morning
when I sit up in bed
I think I can still make it in time.
I dash into my robe,
pick up the phone,
put it down,
look in the closet,
go into the bathroom.

In the mirror I am smoothing my forehead
with my fingers.
I realize you're really dying
and I have never heard
of Sunset Bridge.

My Friends

Millard Buckman

stabbed me
in the fifth grade
with a pencil.
I carry him
in a blue point
in the center of my palm.
We are everywhere,
together.

Millard Buckman [afterword]

Sitting in front of a running electric typewriter on which nothing is being typed can be frustrating. It can also put one to sleep, and at best can hum one into a kind of transcendental meditation. But on this occasion of the droning of the typewriter, I was rubbing my hands and picking at the warts on my fingers, trying to force myself to write a poem. I rubbed my right hand over the permanent blue pencil point in my left hand. FLASH: MILLARD BUCKMAN. FLASH: I'LL NEVER FORGET HIM. FLASH: THE POEM ITSELF, COMPLETED. I typed it out, inspired.

It remains almost as I originally typed it, except for the placement on the page of the last word, *together*. Should the word be on the same line as *everywhere*? Should I put a comma between *everywhere* and *together*? Not until I read the poem aloud for the first time did I decide on its present form.

Together is important. For me that's what a poem does: it brings me together with other people in a different and more intense way than does ordinary speech because in a poem I am better able to show how I react to the world. Perhaps Millard Buckman's act of stabbing me is a better poem than can be written. At least his act will live in his audience of one until his audience dies. The importance of the poem lies in its being able to show a significant aspect of this act to a larger audience. Because of this second act, the poem, I have met literally scores of people who have pencil stains in their bodies and who remember the Millard Buckmans who put them there. Ideally I want every poem to elicit this shock of recognition from a larger audience. In other words my ideal poems would have the MBE—the Millard Buckman Effect.

I have had fantasies of actually meeting Millard Buckman again some day. When I read this poem over the radio I awaited a phone call from him, certain the gods would support this kind of This-Is-Your-Life surprise. I even went to my twenty-year high school class reunion. Not only did he not show, but he had apparently disappeared, despite the astute detective work of the reunion organizers. After all they *did* find me, and I *tried* to be lost. In my most relished fantasy, I assume Millard did not really exist; he was but a spectre come from another world to stab me, to remind me of my mortality, or the power of love and loss. Millard has become a kind of saint in my world: idealized, romanticized, mythologized. And I must confess that the blue point is not really exactly in the center of my palm. That's the difference between art (or should I say religion) and life.

Dream (for Gary C.)

I swim swiftly
from one side of the street
to the other,
push off, push off
from curb to curb,
then glide through the door,
drift up the elevator shaft
to my high dark home.
Everyone's here
to grasp and hug again;
but this time
I feel him
who's always here
and always missing,
as if he's been alive
or dead.
We dance to each other,
chest to chest,
embrace and kiss
till the doorbell rings
below.
　　　　I step
from his arms
through the wall
to see who,
push the pearl button
myself, knock,
ring, and ring.
It's broken and no one is home.
I swim away
bouncing off one wall
then another.

Dream (for Gary C.) [afterword]

Right before I sleep, I sometimes see myself at sunset on a vast curving beach, the brilliant sun firing the sand and my saffron-edged body silhouetted against the dark, redcapped waves. Not only do I see myself, but I become that self and see a ghost as well. It's a Classic Comic ghost: a hooded figure draped in long heavy grey robes with a black hole where his face should be. This ghost, though he makes an undecipherable noise, cannot speak. He comes forward, then recedes, comes forward, then recedes, over and over, from that part of the horizon where there is no sun. This coming and going gets faster and faster until finally the ghost simply becomes part of the endless rhythm of the waves breaking fresh and cold over my bare feet. It has taken me years to realize that the voice of the ghost is really the voice of the waves, the waves that murmur among themselves far out at sea, then shout as they crash against the world, or my toes, pull the sand from under my feet and let me sink.

What does this mean? I'm not sure it means anything. Perhaps it just is (see Archibald MacLeish and John Ciardi). The poem, "Dream," doesn't mean anything either; yet it makes more sense than any rational explanation of my love for a person who was at one time a great and influential presence in my life. He is now a spirit within me who rises and falls and repeats and reminds: one wave among others crashing beautifully over my feet, then pulling me down, getting ready for some future return, until, I suppose, there will be no silhouette blazing on no horizon. Perhaps there will be no beach. Then perhaps the ghost will grow a face and speak.

Except for the placement of the words on the page, this poem is almost as it was when I first wrote it, right after I had the dream.

Judy Lowe

I love to see you, Judy,
once a week, or so.
Your smile is still as young
as it was twelve years ago
when you were twenty-two
and your heart wadded up
like a gum wrapper
despite my love.

Your face is still embarrassed
with freckles,
and your eyes,
lodged in the curve of my skull,
delight me more each year.
I know you love to see me, too.
I think we need each other near.

But I wonder if you should keep coming
to the family swim dream.
Rising out of the pool,
naked, dripping, and wet-eyed,
I find it hard
to explain to the new people
that you're dead.

Judy Lowe [afterword]

Part of the art of poetry is the art of juxtaposing unlike moods, images, ideas, and so forth. In other words the metaphoric mind finds relationships between things that would not be noticed by the rational mind. In this poem there is a juxtaposition of an essentially light and humorous image of the family swim dream followed by a very serious emotion, the recognition of death. I hope the tension between these two emotions creates a new emotion in the reader or listener, the emotion I have in myself that is inexplicable in rational terms.

I tell lies in this poem. Judy was not twenty-two, twelve years ago; but twenty-three, fourteen years ago doesn't sound right.

I got this notion that I could close my eyes and say, "Hey, Judy, come down here and help me explain this poem. After all, we went through a lot. We even went to the senior prom together. Give me a sign." So I closed my eyes, rolled her name over my tongue, silently, as if it were a mantra, and awaited her appearance and reply. But Judy always did have a mind of her own. She appears when she's ready. So it was a futile though common refrain:
   Judy Lowe: (Nothing). Judy Lowe: (Nothing).
   Judy Lowe: (Nothing). (Nothing). (Nothing).

Lee Ann,

Lee Ann,
your black humming
hair
    and wine slick
face; young
        sponge breasts
I plied between two fingers;
lisping eyes;
        grenadine
on the green moon leather carseat;
    where are you?
    we are old.
        Ahh, Lee Ann,
when my wife splits
or dies,
and kids are gone to school forever,
    I'll swim to you
through stars and comets
to South Carolina or California,
and we'll melt
our skins around, burn
old time
on the ghost-green leather,
O Lee Ann, Lee Ann Shafer—
        Scheffer?
I never remember.

Lee Ann [afterword]

"Lee Ann" began as a serious romantic poem, but by the time I finished the first drafts, I felt it was too sentimental. Perhaps, I thought, the poem might end with "we are old" and be able to stand as a serious reverie for days gone by and a sadness about aging; but then a word like *grenadine*, which belies a serious intent, would probably have to be eliminated. With the later addition of the last two lines ("Scheffer?/ I never remember") I rejoiced at having rescued this poem from mediocrity.

As in the previous poem I have also lied in this poem for effect, for a new and different truth: I really *do* remember Lee Ann's last name. A more important fact, however, is that while I might remember her name, I really do *not* remember her as she was. What she was is what I want her to be. Then I realize that some of our emptiness and pain is self-induced, a construct of our own brooding. The next time I begin to brood over the loss of Lee Ann, or some other ancient lover, I shall know better how sweet sorrow can be.

Dear Rick and Ann:

Got your letter today.
To think, I've not even seen your Aaron,
already a year old now.
You live so far;
far away as distant years in my mind.
As far as my kindergarten, where my nose dripped
onto the smooth wooden table, where I rested my head
on crossed arms.
I kept still, afraid of the teacher, who told us not to move.
But that's all I recall about kindergarten in Evansville, Indiana.
What's so special about that?

What will I remember about you after having lived with you
for a year in Copenhagen?
Your smiles? Your eyes, dreamy and romantic
from wearing contacts?
Your excited hands, Ann?
Your clamped brow, Rick, folded—when you were serious—
under your unDanish cap as if you were looking out
from under a rock? And then your easy grin
that opened up your whole face?
Or will I think, years from now, of the cold walk
through the Hermitage; or cooked carrots; the pastries,
like Apple Annie; or Slivovitz at Christmas?
Or the Domkirke at Odense, where Dave Tryggestad blessed us
with Buxtehude from an immense pipe organ,
and we were the only people in that awesome church,
wandering among the pews and altars,
the caps of our skulls coming off with chills?
Yes, I'll remember this, and you, and some of these things.
But I've forgotten so much already.
I remember the nap in kindergarten.

But except for the substitute teacher's mustache in the first grade,
and the wild red hair of my second grade teacher,
I recall nothing but glimpses and shadows
till the third grade:
     In wax paper my mother wrapped a rose
I'd cut from the backyard for a classmate.
I gave it to her after school,
when I caught up to her at the drinking fountain.
She pushed the cast-iron pedal,
drank from the brass fitting
at the center of the silver bowl,
then looked up at me, as she wiped water from her chin
with her palm.
I walked with her past the swings
as far as Keck Avenue,
and never saw her again.

Your letter is still open in front of me,
but soon I'll fold it back into the envelope,
like a rose closed in a book,
like a fold of my mind, darkening, growing blank.

I send my love and a hug (you both do that well)
for Aaron.
Do that for me, for him, who will go to kindergarten
in only four years.

I hope I see you again.
Love,
    Dick

Dear Rick and Ann [afterword]

There is a dome over the ocean of my mind. It is larger than the Arc de Triomphe, larger than the Arch of St. Louis, even larger than the Astrodome. The dome over the mind is like the peephole in your front door through which you are able to see your friends' distorted faces. What if we were unable to open the door, touch them? This poem is about the frustration of being limited by time and space.

Aerogram to a Friend

(Roger Pfingston)

Last week
I taped the snapshots
you made of yourself and other friends
to the kitchen wall.
Because I'm half a world away,
I finally touched you.
And when I did,
your face became a seed,
and a green sprout
curled through my finger,
arm, and neck,
blossomed a strange and lovely garden
in my head.
  I feel you all, daily now,
and each of you is a different flower
I didn't know before.
      Thanks.
Love,
  Dick

Aerogram to a Friend (Roger Pfingston) [afterword]

I had lived all my life either in the hot, sensual forests beside the muddy Ohio river in Southern Indiana, or under the cool skies of Michigan, or through the bright crystalline winters of Minnesota. But this was different. Here I was, alone, wintering in sunless Denmark:

> Small hexagonal tiles on the kitchen sink, large white cold tiles on the wall, thick poured floor, tiny white refrigerator, large casement windows through which weak grey clouds of light barely pass into this small room. No shadows, only dark and darker. It is drizzling as it has been for weeks. Even the oak woodwork feels damp and grey. My eyes ache. I open them wide, try to expand my pupils, close them tight, rub them. I think I am becoming blind. I try to read and become dizzy, so I dream of color, light, lushness, greenness, and Whitman's words that run over and over in my mind like a song that won't let go: "I am mad for it to be in contact with me." It. Whatever it is. Something inside me reaching for warmth, love, for light, for friends. But nothing happens for another week, another week. The toothless grey dog slowly clamps his cold damp gums around my skull.

Out of this madness and a packet of photographs from a friend came the inspiration for "Aerogram"—a poem that reveals one of the reasons why living on alien ground enriches and rewards while it wounds.

Friends

(for John Barnie)

That cold fall day
when we were first together
walking across an empty field,
we saw a wave of sparrows
crash against the grass.
That was beautiful, we said;
and final: the field stood
dead still again
except for our walking.

Yesterday
I was thinking:
now that we must say goodbye,
I would like to leave you as slowly
as a grey winter day.

But I wouldn't
know what to say
sitting there
thinking I should say something
about parting,
my throat corked,
my mind stuck,
the passing time
tearing words
from the corners of my mouth.

I would like to say:
Today
I saw a wave of sparrows
crash against the grass.
But they leapt up again
above the houses and trees
and for an instant
in the upper air
caught fire.

Friends (for John Barnie) [afterword]

Someone asked me what I meant by a "wave of sparrows" crashing against the grass. I was surprised by this question. Another person asked me what I meant about this wave of sparrows catching fire. I was disturbed by this question. Do poets write only for other poets or themselves? Have poets become, like the society in which we live, so specialized that we are virtually irrelevant? Who is our audience? Does it take training to understand the beauty of metaphoric language? Should I explain what I mean by a wave of sparrows? Or why they catch fire in the upper air?

Perhaps it's true, this "catching fire" metaphor might simply be a flash in the pan, sparked by a burning desire to enkindle a warm glow for the finale of the poem. Without flaring up too much about this (and I would prefer not to be so flagrantly flamboyant) I must say that I get fired up with curiosity about people who cannot or will not understand metaphors. Perhaps some people need a blazon of fireworks to light up their lives.

On the other hand maybe fire metaphors are especially difficult to understand.

My Loved Ones

My Brother, Born Dead

(For my mother, with love)

Our mother
felt a gelatin tongue
worm to her womb
from a far mouth
in her brain;

when you dropped,
the cord clung
round your neck.

Dead criminal,
you wrap her now
in invisible lines,
wind her to death.

In nausea days,
when my throat clutches
my breath,
I feel something
circling toward me,
lashing
near the hollows
of my flesh.

My Brother, Born Dead [afterword]

"Nothing begins, and nothing ends,
That is not paid with moan,
For we are born in other's pain,
And perish in our own."
—Francis Thompson
(from "Daisy")

We Are Forcing Forsythia [foreword]

By bringing the unbloomed stems of forsythia inside in late winter, one can "force" them to flower early, but these flowers do not last long.

We Are Forcing Forsythia

We are forcing forsythia
in the cracked churn
that decorates the corner
by the bedroom door.
I fancy,
when I leave the bedroom
of my fresh wife,
that the blossoms draw their yellow
from the butter in the old clay.
And I suppose hard use
once made the crack,
and that things age quickly
like fresh forsythia
forced to
flower.

We Are Forcing Forsythia [afterword]

Poetry is play.
Poetry is building on what has come before.
Poetry is plagiarism.
Poetry is parody.

By bringing in a pound of butter from the refrigerator in late summer, one can "force" it to bloom into a butterchurn in about four days, but these butterchurns do not last long.

We Are Forcing Cracked Butterchurns

We are forcing cracked butterchurns
in the dirty corner
by the bedroom door.
I fancy,
when I leave the bedroom
of my old lady,
that the churns draw their grey
from the grease in the rancid butter.
And I suppose high heat
may have made the mess,
and that long-married couples
must be mad,
like broken butterchurns
obliged to
bloom.

For Sherry

You said you
pulled slim stubborn silks
for hours
from strawberry popping corn,
then blew the hulls
to get a good clean kettle full.
When we married,
your hands
were sure,
your mouth,
tart strawberry,
so oval O.
I loved you:
tight food in the seed;
and now,
as our family flowers with children
and with years,
I know you must have seen
the hulls, too,
flashing for a moment in the sun
like the fingers
from this garden sprinkler:
arcs and webs
of luminous beads.

For Sherry [afterword]

Things

Our shining white wedding Volkswagen
slouches down with splayed fenders
on fat airless tires.
My allergenic wedding band
hides in the bottom drawer
of a house years away.
And, remember? You
turned my coin collection
to cigarettes one winter:
their old dates, figures, and faces
still clink up a pillar of smoke,
become bright moons in my dreams;
but I can't quite grab them back.
This morning I stuffed the drooping cluster
of pink and white carnations
down the garbage disposal:
I only gave them to you Tuesday.
What gives with all these things
that woo our love then fall apart
or disappear?

Now look:
What if I hold out
my empty upturned hand
and ask you to know
the thing it holds;
could you,
without seeing or touching
whatever it might be,
could you look me in the eyes
and by saying nothing,
say *Yes*?

Things [afterword]

Occasionally when I try to write, my brain is cluttered with all sorts of irrelevancies. Anyone who meditates understands what I say. Some days your mind refuses to stay on the mantra, and you find yourself thinking about what John and Mary said, about what you're going to have for supper, about whose turn it is to pick up the kids from school, and about not being able to write or meditate.

Like the most satisfying meditations, I believe the best poetry is frequently written when the mind is not actively thinking. At least poems do not often come, for me, when I think about poetic ideas. I rarely say, "Now, let's see, what shall I write about." Rather, I seem to have to enter into a state of nonthinking (like the meditator) for ideas worth writing about to surface. In this state the mind is relaxed and seems to shoot straight through to some calm center, some womb where the day's trash is at least 'back there"—in a sometimes-frenetic other-consciousness.

This poem is about those things in the real wide-awake world that, for many people, provide the only definition of their existence. Obviously we *are* defined by the material things we push before us, or drag behind us, or place around us. This poem only wants to say that there is something more, something positive that is not material, some communication that is not verbal, some togetherness that is not physical, does not depend on the trash, the effluvia, the clutter, but that shoots right through these to something that might, yes, be called love.

Marital Bliss

Sometimes
when life seems but spaces
between dog hairs—
in my meatloaf, milk, and mouth—
I daydream
of dogless, childless, empty rooms.
Just you and me
filling spaces
between kisses and embraces:
suck, fuck, sweat, and shower,
unable to tell week from hour.

And so tonight,
fifteen years later,
when this long day is almost gone
and you stride from your hot shower,
glistening in your pink skin
across the living room
to the bedroom,
I get an itch,
and stalk your delectable ass,
rising up
like a flare
out of our domestic
dogpound.

Marital Bliss [afterword]

(a middle-aged romantic love poem with 2 gratuitous fourletter
words, *fuss* and *ack*)

In a forty-five-minute reading I gave that was taped and later broad-
cast over a University radio station in 1977, this poem, and only this
poem, was cut from the reading. It must be worth reading.

Here are some variations for radio stations:
 suck, censor, sweat, and shower . . .
 and stalk your delectable censor. . . .

or
 suck, f———, sweat, and shower . . .
 and stalk your delectable a———. . . .

or
 suck, beep, sweat, and shower . . .
 and stalk your delectable beep. . . .

or
 suck, fuss, sweat, and shower . . .
 and stalk your delectable ack. . . .

Nobody Will Talk About My Poem [foreword]

There are many morbid poets. In fact one wonders, sometimes, if one of the prerequisites for being a poet is preoccupation with death, disease, and decay. At least one can say that anyone who is serious about living, as most poets are, is certainly concerned about death.

This poem reveals one of the ways in which a self might react to the fear of, the prospect of, the death of a loved one. It has the added feature of being in very bad taste, like death itself.

The poetry of Eberhart, Silkin, Jarrell, Wilbur (their names, spoken, become a poem) can easily endure a tongue-in-cheek parody such as this.

Nobody Will Talk About My Poem

You found a lump in your breast,
then went to Canada
for a preplanned weekend conference.

I went to pieces:
I hung up my clothes,
as if for once it mattered.
I bought you a half gallon
of your favorite peppermint soap,
then wondered if you'd last that long.
I made the bed,
and before I washed your dirty clothes,
I held them to my nose.
And then, when I could do nothing more,
I, like every morbid poet,
got the urge to enshrine this disaster
with a poem.

Poets are strange that way.
You've heard their audiences talk after readings:

> "Did you hear that great poem
> about being hosed out of the cockpit?"

> "Did you hear the one
> about his son who died?
> Wasn't that some poem?"

> "What about the one
> where his pet groundhog
>   got run over by a truck?
> Wow!"

But nobody will talk about my poem.
Cause here you are.
Still around.
Wondrously benign.

Omen

In the morning
my brain cramped, body coiled,
as if salt flowed through my skull
to knot the slug inside.
This, because at breakfast,
before he skipped off to kindergarten,
my son surmised,
with a thoughtful gaze,
"Today you are going to die."

His spirit's as clean as a prophet's
or a yogi-saint's;
eyes are charged from within;
palms have the right lines;
the sun curls at ease in his hair.
And when he's serene, the Universe, surprised,
quivers around him, like a lake dances
around a buoy.
Is this just the Father projecting the Son?
I didn't die.
But the clock grinded like a rusted joint.
My body's cells burned,
and my thoughts fluttered
like ashes.
How my lungs rejoiced at midnight!
And the following dawn
I shouted gratitude beyond the stratosphere.

All morning I intercepted the smile of the sun
and returned the waves of the dancing trees.
But by noon, the day was ablaze,

and I loosened my tie against the deadening heat.
Afternoon, I forgot a prayer of thanks
at coffeebreak.
Before supper, I downed too many beers;
and in the evening,
I kicked a stray dog from the garage,
and stumbled out the garbage cans
for the rusty truck
that roars
and eats us up
in the morning.

Omen [afterword—a short sermon]

After crises pass most of us, relieved, resolve to better ourselves, better
our relationships with our loved ones, and live our remaining days
more richly and fully. So we change our lives for a day or two, then
slip back into the pattern of drudgery out of which, through fear, we
were temporarily awakened. But for one critical moment we came
closer to finding out about our Self in relation to our life and death,
and for another critical moment we were able to enjoy what we learned.
Yet we return to the beer, the anger at the dog, and the garbage cans.
Do we simply have short memories? Are we lazy? Does our American
culture disallow such excursions into the Self? Yes, to all three ques-
tions. In our culture of throwaways, junk food and clothes, trash TV
and toys, and popularity contests, we are begged to escape from excur-
sions into our Selves, from finding out who we really are—Selves who
are afraid and insecure; Selves curious and alive with questions and
doubts; Selves striving for completion and fulfillment. The new God is
an Adman who tells us we can put aside our death by buying a new car
or watching the latest jiggle show. And indeed it is true: our material-
istic society does offer palliatives to the yearning Soul. But like most
stop-gaps they become, like Demerol, addictive, till we find we need
more and *bigger*, till matter replaces spirit instead of complementing it.
Money becomes the means by which we hope to pay off Mr. D.; so we
push and shove and scramble for the bottom line, which tallies up as
"$," or "The New Christ," or "No Death," or "Jiggle Show"—they
are all the same. Perhaps we need to find a different Christ, a Christ
that—however we choose to define her—is within us, trying to be
recognized.

For My Son

Tonight before he went to bed
he curled upon the stairs
and wept.
Yesterday he said goodbye to his friend.
This morning, hurling a tennis ball
at the siding, over and over,
he wished to collapse our house,
be free of his pain.
She's moving to Buffalo.

I hugged him,
said nothing,
my body filling up with partings:
    the rose I gave Kitty Cissel
    who got TB in my 3rd grade;
    Mother, Father, Judy Lowe, John,
    whom I hugged;
    Calvin, and more, and more.

Severn, my son,
9 years old,
this poem is for you,
because in time
we want to keep
from losing
everything.

For My Son* [afterword]

Few of us are good parents. We try to become parents while we are parenting. But one gesture has made a difference in our family: the reaching out of the hand, the touch.

The artist tries to achieve the magic of touch in music, or poems, or novels, or painting, or sculpture. Perhaps great art is the expression of the joy of touch coupled with the pain of recognition that physical touch cannot last.

----

*Kitty Cissel (see "Dear Rick and Ann"), Father (see "Sunset Bridge"), Judy Lowe (see "Judy Lowe"), John (see "Friends"), Calvin (see Forbes's *Blue Monday*), Severn (see "Omen" and "Log Slide Dune").

Nikstlitslepmur

(For Caeri, my 4-year-old daughter,
who said, "Let's read it backwards tonight.")

The dwarf sprang cursing
from the ground,
then smiled and danced.
The queen said, "Mot, Kcid.
No, Sgelredips, or Rapsac."
But she finally resigned herself
to stuffing her child
back into her womb.
Then she quit the king
for a tower
where the dwarf gave her a ring,
a necklace, and rooms full of straw
from gold.
Then her father, the Miller, said,
"Straw of out gold spin
can who daughter a
have I."
Then they were poor and unhappy,
normal.

Nikstlitslepmur [afterword]

Often children are able to intuit the joys of difference better than adults, who, once they become comfortable with a task, do it unconsciously, routinely, with drudgery. How often have you enjoyed watching your hands perform the physical miracle of tying your own shoes?

Eyes open with even, asleep fast fall we soon and, growth no be can there, change without for, perspective our alter is ourselves for do can we things important most the of one.

Log Slide Dune, Lake Superior

Stunned though we were at that height,
we could clearly see the sand ledge drop off
a hundred yards out,
the clear blue widen into the sky.
Then, having never seen a dune before,
our kids pranced and tumbled to the bottom,
sand flying from their heels and hands
like skydivers leaving a trail.
Our hearts with them,
we followed, much slower,
only dreaming what we used to do.

At the bottom
they greeted us with shining stones,
purple and white, an agate here, perhaps.
"Maybe a pearl!" whooped our son.

We looked for gems
while they played up and down the dune.
Our son sprinted back and forth along the beach;
the wet sane seemed to spring him on.
Our daughter,
darting in and out of the cold water
that sprayed around her feet,
suddenly stopped,
threw out her arm,
turned her small eyes to the horizon,
and worried, "Are sharks here?"
I was rubbing a smooth flat stone.
"Not here," I said, then flung it out for seven skips
before it sank.

"Good," she sighed,
then scampered half way up then down the dune again.

Soon,
my arm sore,
my wife's back cramped from bending over rocks,
the kids furious at having to leave just now,
we started up.
The sun was hotter.
The breeze stopped.
The kids ran ahead, cackled at us,
and kicked sand that stuck like gnats
to our sunburnt faces.
We dug steps, walked backwards,
to ease our aching calves and shins.

Halfway up,
the kids haranguing us from the top,
sand fleas and deer flies biting,
our pockets bulging with shoebox treasures,
we stopped,
watched each other heave and sweat,
wondering of all things if we should have done this.
Together we turned,
leaned our backs against the steep sand,
the bright, impossible Superior lying before us;
and the only sharks were inching up our veins
toward the pounding of our weakening hearts.

Log Slide Dune, Lake Superior [afterword]

In my study I can leap from the crest of the dune and soar out over the lake, so high that the air in my lungs is thin.
I become giddy, and I see my family—small, naked figures cupped in the dune's giant cove.
My tiny daughter points her arm out to sea, and there, my son sprints faster than seems possible along the beach.
My wife, a few feet away into the clear water is a speck squatting among the smooth stones like a child again.
And I am also there, standing on the dark cool lip of sand between the water and the hot dune, watching.
I am watching my wife, woman, mother, full breasts flattened against her knees, become the painting of a ripe pear among the liquid stones.
And I am answering my lovely, worried daughter, a statue pointing to some end, silhouetted against the bright white bend of the dune.
And I am shielding my eyes to see, behind her, my lean, muscular son, caught in a photograph, his legs a blur, except, barely touching the sand, the ball of one foot, under which sunlight glints.
Now I am wheeling my head slowly away from my family, look out over the Superior, and become startled for a moment to see that I am looking at myself, hovering high over the lake, over this vast distance of time and space.
We accept each other as one and the same, the same also as he who sits in his study conjuring, and the same also as he who writes about the great gift of life that is sometimes captured in art:

mystery.

My Self

My Self [foreword to the entire section]

In this section the poems have been arranged into a kind of mini-book to reveal the brief excursion of a persona through doubts about the meaning and significance of his personal life, and his "enlightenment" into becoming a "poet," which, because of his new vision, allows him to accept reality.

The arrangement here, as in most books of poems, is designed to enhance the combined strength of individual poems, and is secondary to each individual poem, which has its intrinsic merit without *having* to rely on the poems preceding or following it. Novelists usually do a much better job of developing stories and plots, because for them the form of the whole book is the shape of the content, whereas for the poet the form of each poem is the shape of the content. The best book of poems would express both of these qualities.

The whole Self has at least two parts: the sun side and the moon side. We are all familiar with the sun side, because we use it most in our western world to "get along" in the world "out there." In terms of the yin/yang, the sun side is the masculine, ratiocinative, and logical, whereas the moon side is the feminine and intuitive. When I think of my poet-Self, I think of the moon side, that mysterious 90 percent of my brain that is not my conscious sun side.

The western world does not like to recognize this dark, intuitive, feminine side of the self. Most westerners operate in the world as if the most important things in life take place in the full light of day when they are totally conscious, perhaps trying to figure out some problem, logically. I believe most poets, while they are of course conscious human beings (in most cases), are in touch with that dark side of the self from whence comes mystery, metaphor, ambiguity, and intuition. This section reveals that preoccupation with the moon side of the whole self.

I'd like to tell a short story about how these poems came into being, because it helps illustrate the way the moon side of the self works.

John Dolphin

A very good friend of mind, John Dolphin, has also been my mentor in revealing to me the secrets of the metaphoric mind. John is an exceptional teacher because he is at home with both, or should I say *all*, aspects of the self. He has helped me immensely in breaking through the different layers of the self to arrive at other places. And in these different places he has introduced me to some very charming and sympathetic characters, two of whom you may know: Papatkin and Boethigm. On one particular occasion, when my vision seemed especially narrow (I felt as if I were looking at reality through the core of a roll of paper towels), John crashed through one side of this tube, wriggled his body very ostentatiously, and then crashed out the other side. Fortunately he had taught me how to see beyond the tunneled vision, so I was able, after some effort, to follow him into other space, and indeed, ultimately, even over the high white buildings of New York where, in an unforgettable sunset, John, from my vantage point, seemed to metamorphose into a giant, golden, prehistoric dragonfly, until with a quick flip of his glistening tail, he skirted around to the back of my head and plunged headlong into the dark sea.

Remarkable about this particular plunge of John's were the poems that splashed up around his body. Beautiful darkred poems gleaming in the sunset. Handfulls of them. Naturally I wanted to preserve them before the sun actually set, for I knew, at that time they would be lost, not only to me, but to the world, forever.

Without prolonging this story more than is necessary, let me simply conclude by saying that I *was* able to gather a small bundle of these poems, whereupon I ran home skipping and smiling through the fields with the thought of presenting these beautiful gifts to my young and sensual mother. These will make her happy, I thought. These will make

both of us happy. She was waiting for me at the door of our small
cabin on the hill, her radiant smile, her yellow hair, her white apron,
and her open arms reflecting the dying rays of the soft, mellow sun.

>Behind her
>on the other side of the doorway,
>the inside of the house
>was black.

And that's the end
of the story
of how John Dolphin
is responsible
for the poems
in this section.

Myself, My Home, The Moon

I am pale at my intersection,
the intersection is pale,
and the houses
along my street
gleam
like empty hospitals.

In a bed of white grass,
my house,
where I find myself, again,
falling on the front door,
jamming keys at the hole.

But tonight
part of me has slipped to the backyard,
where I unfold an aluminum lawn chair,
sit, hum,
and listen
to my squeaking teeth—strange
keyboard
for the schizophrenic moon.

The Dream

Stone,
the moon pushes me to bed.
The rain circle
a half-opened eyelid,
holds the sky.
I dream the glistening mountains,
the rock where we lie
naked on rough shadows.
You bend your head back
to the round belly of the universe
and I become
the rock and rough,
the lizard and frog,
the slumber of my touch,
the death of my hand,
jerking helplessly,
a beached whale
under the gentle
measured closing
of your eye.

This Office

Over here is my window.
It is one solid sheet of thermalglass.
It doesn't open.
Above are my fluorescent lights.
Here is my empty Coke can.
Here, an empty styrofoam coffeecup.
Here, a Tab.
This drawer contains aspirin
and Preparation H;
this one, instant soup.
Here's a stapler and tape.
Behind me are my books: 10 rows, 2 deep.
There, a trash can:
the gum wrapper stuck to the black guck
is from the last person in this office.
The guck is from 1965.
The trash can, the desk,
the stapler, the tape dispenser,
the in-and-out trays, the filing cabinet,
the floor, the walls, the bookcases—these
are all grey.
I think the books are grey too.
It is snowing,
the first snow this winter.
Some of the white flakes float up to my window,
stop, as if to peer in,
then hurry away.

The Awakening

1.
Every night I pray
my back will be better
in the morning.
In the morning I pray the same.

2.
Stepping from the shower
I see the wet spot on the floor
where my arch should have been.

3.
After shaving
I pick at the sebacious cysts
on my forehead
till they bleed.

4.
I unroll my socks over my legs
where blue veins lie like thick worms.

5.
I've got a Wrinkle-Guard Dryer
for my clothes,
but my body's getting worse.

6.
Patches of my retina
are mutilated
or dead.
I can tell by the holes I see
when I close my eyes.

In dreams I pass through these.

On Reincarnation
and Related Matter

If a deathless spirit
sticks in these bones,
flows in this blood,
where does it show itself?
In the gnarl of my fingers?
In the feel of my feet
against the ground?
In the way the skin falls
around my eyes?
Does spirit wait to be coddled
or cudgeled
from a hideout in my head?
Do I turn a poem with Beethoven's wrist?
or hear with a John Smith ear?
It's easy enough to tap the cask
to get the wine,
but how do we tap a body
to pour the light?

A Poem

At the base of my back
it rises like bruised water
begun to swell;
it climbs my spine,
deposits clover in every bone,
and each stamen sprays
a thousand tiny mad bees
under my skin.
It pushes higher
into my head
like dark fog
piling up on a field of grass.
Then it gathers in a cold silver pool
and spills, like dew
from the cup of a flower,
down my arms, chest, and legs.
                              I am
sitting on stone.
                    I am
folding inside myself.
                         I am
I am.

Poets

One might slip into your mind by night,
like suicide;
another, scatter pink petunias in your path;
and yet another, surprise you
sliding a knife over his lips
to sputter bloody flowers.
I stand before you as I am
to show you what I know.

See those gauze curtains raise their arms?
Feel the breeze run its cool hands
over the formica tabletop,
drop to the floor,
circle your legs,
then climb the backs of your arms
to your neck?
See that marvelous light
make stars of the few particles of dust?
It's so bright,
I can barely see the apples
on the tree outside,
or the cars on the street behind,
or the telephone wires,
or the men and women.
But I *can* see them
through this window.

I'm not possessed;
no more than you are
by this harsh light
(see it?)
that warms us,
chills us,
holds us
all.

The Soft Repose of Is

The smell of soup
warms me at the front door.
Soapy steam from the shower
caresses the house after supper.
My daughter cuddles
and my son sings himself
to sleep.

No coming.
              No going.

Simply the downy pillow,
the comforter fallen over my chest,
the quick rise
and slow falling
of my finger
as I drift
away.

Frog Praises Night

"My friend,
you have made black pearls
of my eyes,
and my tongue is a silk fork
for the spice-wet stars
in your hair."

Frog Praises Night [afterword]

My friends, my loved ones, my self: they are all the same.

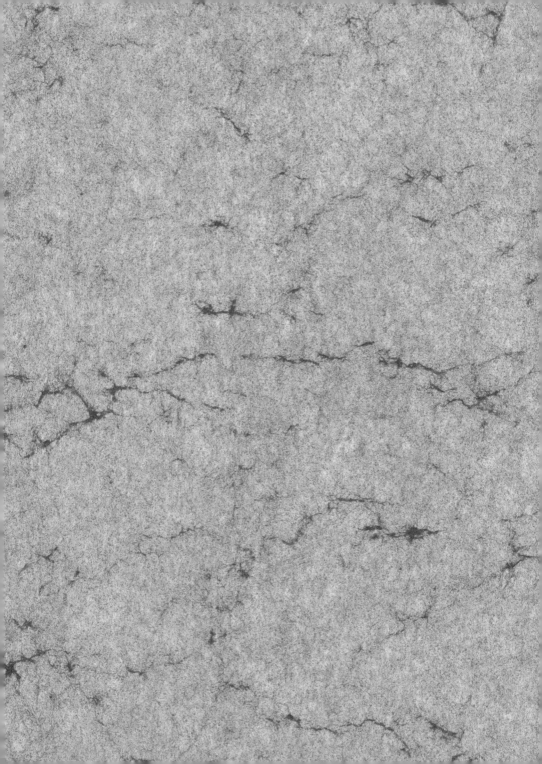